AF413134

FALLING

Falling

DAWN SOLIS

CONTENTS

COPYRIGHT

DEDICATION

To those who are waiting for a love like a stained glass window

PREFACE

This collection goes through my poems surrounding love. *However loose that definition may be.* So, whether you are falling in love or falling from a cliff that you thought was love, this poetry collection is for you.

~ 1 ~

DROWNING

She fell in love, but there was nobody to catch her.
She fell with reckless abandon.
She fell as Icarus fell away from the sun.
She smiled as she imagined the soft water enveloping her,
soothing her aching heart, smoothing the wrinkles in between her
brows and running its soft finger through her hair.
Instead-
She gets a current as hard as a rock,
Her lip busts and her heart breaks, but she waits.
I'll get away from the cliff.
The waves will be kinder.
The harder she tries to swim the harder the current pulls her
apart.
Her tears mix with the salty ocean.
It's my fault. She thinks.
I'm the one who jumped.
The ocean never promised me anything.
Just because it was beautiful and soft on the beach doesn't mean that it
promised to be kind forever.
She tries to fight but the more she moves the harder it pushes.
It's so dark.
She sucks in a breath of water.

This is for the best.
I'm the one that put myself in this situation.
Just as she goes to suck in another breath and accept her fate,
arms go under hers, and she can finally see the sky. The
beautiful blue sky.
And the man that holds it in his eyes.

~ 2 ~

REVENGE

I hope you feel disgusted with yourself when you look in the
mirror.
I hope your body rolls with grief when someone with auburn hair
catches your eye.
I hope you raise a man just like you, so you can watch him repeat
the same mistakes you made.
I hope you loathe yourself, because of how deeply my love ran for
you.
I hope you hate yourself as much as I hate you for loving me.

~ 3 ~

BREAKING ME

I never thought you would be the one to break my heart.
You, with a soft smile and warm heart.
You, with the gentle promises and whispered reassurances.
But you did.
You broke me.
You swept my feet out from underneath me and pretended to catch me,
reaching out your arms.
But as my back hits the dust and the air is knocked out of my lungs,
you shrug.
I gasp in a breath, asking why, coughing against the dusty truths in my mouth,
and you do not have an answer.
I never thought you would be the one to break my heart,
but you did.
You broke it into so many pieces that I had no choice but to leave the holes there,
and patch them closed with cold concrete.
A transplant of warm love to a cold destruction of my own soul.
You broke me.

~ 4 ~

RAZOR WIRE

I string razor wire through my rib cage so that other people
can't do it first.
If I pierce my own heart, it doesn't hurt as bad when others sink
the knife deeper.
Hurting yourself makes it hurt less when others inflict harm.

~ 5 ~

SHAME

I string razor wire through my rib cage so that other people
can't do it first.
If I pierce my own heart, it doesn't hurt as bad when others sink
the knife deeper.
Hurting yourself makes it hurt less when others inflict harm.

$$\sim 6 \sim$$

CAN WE START OVER?

Can we start over?
I know that we are both broken.
I know that last time, we both destroyed each other.
But,
can we start over?
Surely two broken hearts can make one whole one.
Can we start over and do it right?
Can we start over and fix what we broke?
Or will we both constantly live with the guilt that comes from
never knowing what could have been?

~ 7 ~

TRUST

They tell me that I can trust them,
Of course my first response is no.
I have learned the hard way that even the kindest people are liars
when it comes to me.
No one stays unless forced to by societal obligations.
I am convinced that if my mother saw me on the street she would
wrinkle her nose in disgust.
My father scoffs at my friends when they are a reflection of my
inner soul,
my brother rolls his eyes when he listens to my mind spin.
They love me I know that was never in the question.
I have learned the hard way that being loved and being liked are
two different things.
They tell me that I can trust them,
I nod my head and move on with my day but I know,
oh gods above do I know how terrible it is to be lied to.

~ 8 ~

RED STRING THEORY

There is a feeling of wanting to be home. A line drawn from the
center of your chest to a far away distance.
A feeling where you *know* there is a place your being comes alive,
where you *know* you can lay your head to rest, where you *know*
your soul can rest.
I ache for it.
I know he will break my heart without knowing his last name.
I want to be able to say *when* I get married, instead of if,
I grew up thinking that every person finds their person, their
place.
But I learned as I matured that some people die alone, traveling a
path with no destination in sight.
Some people never get to speak vows. Some speak vows and break
them.
I want to say *when* I find my place, my love,
instead of if.
I wonder why I am broken.
I fear that I will forever be homeless, lost and confused,
stumbling in this loneliness on this path called life.
One half of an empty soul. Of an empty home.

~ 9 ~

BRUISES AND BROKEN SOULS

I still have that blanket your mother gave me for my 17th birth-
day.
The paper cranes that you painstakingly made for me sit, dusty at
the top of my closet. I look at them but do not touch them.
Do you still side eye me the way I side eye you?
Just to check, for bruises and broken souls.
I crave for the dirty side of a broken love song but do you wish me
ill?
I wonder if your favorite food has changed.
Mine has, surely yours has too.
We are different people than we were then.
Does that make our love a fake disaster all over again?

~ 10 ~

KISS ME

Kiss me as if you care for me
Kiss me as if you look at me and see beauty
Kiss me as if I am not a piece of meat on your way to something
more long lasting
Kiss me as if I am not a stranger
Kiss me as if you actually care what I have to say

~ 11 ~

STRANGULATION

I am so desperate for love that I strangle it in an attempt to hold
on. Three deleted texts, and a fourth one that reads 'never mind'.
I want to collect scraps of you:
Your birthday,
Your middle name,
The freckle on the inside of your arm and the stretch marks on
your back from puberty when you grew too fast.
I hold the universe in a death grip, whispering threats into igno-
rant ears while I *beg* them to let me keep this one, keep you.
I have never loved like this before I silently scream inside.
I hear a faint laughing as you hold my hand, reverberated by the
sound of a ticking clock.

~ 12 ~

FALLING

Commitment is a chair, and as I start to settle in, the words, I'm
in love with my ex, rings through the air.
And the seat vanishes from beneath me, allowing me to fall back
onto the floor, where I am comfortable.
Safe
Steady
No shaky legs or wobbly bolts.
No second glances or trembling lips.
Commitment is a chair, and I would rather sit on the cold lonely
ground, than fall again.

~ 13 ~

LOVE STORY

A poem dedicated to my Grandparents, Teresa and Ricardo Solis.
Slow down
Calm your heart and mind and your soul
Until we
Slow to a standstill
Until the only sound is our hearts, beating in sync but not in
rhythm
Until the only sight is your beautiful eyes
Until our souls collide
Rest your brow on mine and intertwine the tips of our fingers until
all you can hear is my breathing in your perfume,
out my worries
Until your vision shifts and your feet go numb from swaying back
and forth with me
Slow down
Until we become one

~ 14 ~

REDEFINED

Love yourself more than anyone could have ever dreamed of
loving you.
Drag your fingertips down your own skin, marveling at the
bumps and scars that are proof you are alive.
Kiss your own shoulder as you bathe in the warm sunlight.
Look in the mirror and tell yourself that you are glorious.

~ 15 ~

VALUE ME

"You deserve someone who values you." He states,
breaking,
cleaving
destroying
my heart in two.
"You... don't value me?" I whisper, not being able to wrap my
mind around how this is actually happening right now.
He told me he loved me.
He told me he wanted to marry me, and wanted me to take his
last name.
But now as I stand here in the cold and the wet I realize it was
all a figment of my imagination.
"I do-just not enough for me to continue this relationship. I'm
sorry."
Sorry.
He's sorry.
Broken promises fill the air around us as my head swims.
It's my fault. I realize.
I trusted him.
I loved him.
This is all my fault.

~ 16 ~

I WANT

I want an Icarus and the sun type of love.
I want a love that is dangerous.
So full of passion and adoration that we break and mend each
other like the wax on Icarus wings.
I want him to adore my hands.
For him to kiss the scar on my knuckle that no one has noticed
before .
I want to watch him cry over the scars that his father has left on
his heart.
The ones that no one has ever noticed,
I want a love that is all encompassing,
All consuming,
Everlasting,
I want a love like Icarus and the sun.

~ 17 ~

WAITING FOR MY LOVER

A lack of love makes you hard.
The longer that my heart beats for only my craft the more
calloused it becomes.
My hands turn to claws as I wait to run it down a lover's face.
The problem with licking love off of knives is that sometimes you
mistake your own blood for poison.

~ 18 ~

FROM A LOVER TO ANOTHER

You are not worthless because you are treated less,
You are worthy of love and kindness and affection,
And if someone does not give that to you then that shows their
own misconception of the world.
You are amazing and kind and you deserve what the world has to
offer.
You will bloom,
And flower,
And prosper.

~ 19 ~

BEING OPEN

My voice is not sweet like honey.
My lips do not taste like plums.
My skin is not soft like the butterflies wing.
My laugh will grate against your ears like sandpaper.
I know why people do not read my words,
I am not someone who is made for the light.
But as I sit in the darkness I can't help but imagine,
being a person that someone wishes to listen to.

~ 20 ~

PERFECTIONISM IS TORMENT

I want someone to love me first. Before anything else.
Selfishly
Toxicity
Brokenly
I think it is the perfectionist in me.
Wanting to be the winner of everything all of the time,
it is blatant insecurity.
A terror that no coloring books or soft pillows will fix.
The little girl that lives inside of me stomps her feet.
What a terrible thing, to love someone just because they wish to
have a medal placed around their neck.

~ 21 ~

LOVING LIKE EDGAR

I don't care if you love me so,
I will rot in my woes,
And write my thoughts down just like Poe.
I am my own foe,
And I don't ever know
Just when death will say hello.
But maybe you will love me so,
Until I go.

~ 22 ~

I BEG NOTHING OF YOU

"What do you want from me?" A snapped sentence. A terrified
soul.
"Nothing." A soft confession. A broken promise.
"Nothing?" An asked question. A stopped heart.
He shakes his head softly, as if too much movement will scare me
away. It probably will.
"Just your love." A soft whisper pointed toward the ground.
A sudden breaking.
I realize I can't breathe. Because that's something I've been trying
to give him for years.

~ 23 ~

MIRACLE CURE

Do you think that love can fix me?
Feelings take up space, arms raise to straighten rib cages.
I, too, wish to take up enough space to open someones arms.
Do you think the sea would fix me?
I love selfishly, I take and take-
Until you have nothing left to give.
I fear that I will have a thousand loves but never be called *wife*.
Do you think the sun will renew me?
I plug my soul in so that it may recharge.
I skip meals, not on purpose, I just open my eyes and I can
count the rib bones that press against my skin from the inside.
I've lost days.
Do you think that love will fix me?

~ 24 ~

REACHING OUT

I am clinging to the side of a cliff.
My knuckles turn white and my biceps are shaking with the force
of holding my mind above the darkness that lays below me.
I always thought that hell was fiction, but as I spare a glance at the
abyss below me I realize that it is real.
All too real.
So when you put a hand over the edge and help to pull me up, I
don't hesitate to scramble for you,
To get help,
To get out,
To finally feel alive again,
To not be afraid.
But then your grip starts to slip and I realize that you weren't
trying to help me you were just trying to be the hero.
You never loved me.
But now it's too late.
I can't grab the edge of the cliff now, I can't do anything else but
put my faith in you.
And as I scream at you to *please just pay attention* and get me out of
here,
You let your hand relax, and I fall.

~ 25 ~

I DON'T HATE YOU

I don't hate you
I hate the reflection that you are
You reflect the insecurities that broil inside of me
When I look at you I see my crooked nose
I see my hateful smile
I see my terrible demeanor
I see my own darkness
So no
I don't hate you
I just truly hate myself

~ 26 ~

WONDERS AND BROKEN
PROMISES

I speak to myself worse than I speak to my enemies.
I went to war for you and all you saw was paper cuts.
I feel as if I deserve it.
After all of these years if I am still the one in the dirt I can't help
but wonder if I was made to be there.
I wonder what you told her,
I wonder if you held her hand as you told her we just weren't
compatible,
or if you raked your teeth down her neck as you spoke of the
horrific details of how my heart was broken by your hands.
Anyway it doesn't matter.
It never did.
You gave me a bite and I tried to be satisfied as if it was the whole
meal.
I wonder if her appetite is less than mine or if you made the serv-
ings larger for her.
Was it just not enough? Or is she too much?
I hate this, this comparison of two women who don't even know
each other.
Yet I can't help but wonder what you told her,
I still speak to myself worse than I speak to my worst enemies.

~ 27 ~

AGGRESSION

I can't have love without aggression.
I tell my best friend that my dream guy is a man who will snap at
me, tell me to shut up and sit down when I mouth off too much. I
find comfort in the fact that one day I might find someone who I
can't push too far. I find comfort in the fact that maybe one day I
will find someone who will be as aggressive towards me as I am to
myself.
I portray it as romance.
She cocks her head to the side and says, "Do you want something
toxic?" Confusion mars her face, probably thinking back to her
love, how gentle and sweet it is.
I giggle, telling her, "It's not toxic. It's masculine. It's strength."
"Do you know the difference?"
My answer can only be no.

~ 28 ~

FAILURE

To the man who made me believe in love again:
I tell you you are my whole world, my head against your chest.
Silence envelopes us, your chest stops moving and I look up to
watch as a furrow begins in between your brows, deep and pain-
ful.
A tear begins in the corner of your lashes, collecting in the hollow
of your eyes, not traveling down the high curve of your cheek-
bones
My heart breaks for the boy that you were as I hold you against my
sternum as you wipe your tears on the hem of my sweatshirt.
No wonder you love so hard, because you had never felt love
before.

~ 29 ~

LITERATURE

Promises promises
Your words turn to dust, ashes in my mouth.
Promises promises,
The world stops spinning.
I don't believe in literature anymore

AUTHOR'S NOTE

Ever since I have been a little girl I have felt as if I have had a warped view on love. It wasn't until I got a little older and realized that *everyone* has a warped view on love.

Once, a guy asked me why I was single. I said "I refuse to lick love off knives".

I realized very early on that there is such a thing called love, but it isn't what it seems like. I grew up thinking that my grandparents had the ultimate love story (just like everyone else's grandparents). Then I got older, and I realized that they had problems too, challenges too, the only difference is that they chose to stay. They both stayed. Regardless of how hard it was. Isn't that the real definition of love? Staying even when it's hard, and messy? My parents had the same story. No matter how hard it got, or how many troubles they went through, they both chose to stay. They realized their love was stronger than the storm they were facing. I realize that this isn't everyone's story. Some have to leave, regardless of how much they love their partner. Love stories don't always have a happy ending.

This collection goes through my poems surrounding love. However loose that definition may be. So, whether you are falling in love or falling from a cliff that you thought was love, this poetry collection is for you.